*Dedicated to Dawn, whose passion and dedication for
natural dog care inspired me along my animal healing journey.
For which I will always be grateful.*

Published by Love, Woof and Wonder Publishing
United Kingdom, 1st Edition, 2012

Text and images Copyright © Caroline Griffith
with the exception of pages 40/41 Copyright Jez Rose and pages 42/43 copyright Bob Weatherwax.
Cartoon images Copyright © Andy Nash

Anatomy Diagrams with thanks to Hope Turner FdSc Canine Health 101

Forward

Caroline has produced a very concise, informative and easy to read manual that will help the novice and stimulate the veteran raw-fooder. This book will help all dog owners to a greater understanding of their dog, their dog's digestion and how best to cater for them.

The problem with beginning to feed raw is that there is just too much information, opinion and prejudice out there to know where to start. Opinions are like noses; everyone has one. And everyone is sure that they have the answer. The truth is that many of them have good ideas that can help your dog. No one has all the answers for your particular dog, but you can enjoy trying different approaches to find the system that works best.

I see dogs at my practice every day that benefit from raw food. Some are very sick, some are supposedly 'healthy' on processed food; all of them benefit from the change from factory food to a well-crafted raw diet. As Caroline says, all dogs, like all humans, are different. In time, you will find tweaks to the general advice that suit your dog better; in astronomy they call this the Goldilocks zone – neither extreme, but just right for your dog at their particular time of life.

We are told by our doctors to avoid processed foods. If you think about it, even prisoners, astronauts and soldiers at war are not subjected to 'scientifically balanced', biologically inappropriate dehydrated or tinned foods repeated ad nauseam for months and months, years and years. Somehow, we have been brainwashed into thinking that this is ok for dogs.

Read this short book. You will learn a little or a lot about your dog. And they will be grateful for it, in their own happy way.

Nick Thompson BSc (Vet Sci) Hons,
BVM&S, VetMFHom, MRCVS

www.holisticvet.co.uk

3

Contents

Canis Lupus Familiaris

No matter whether you own a pure bred Chihuahua, a big Great Dane, a soppy Staffie, a loopy but lovable Labrador or like my dog a Whattie (a we're not quite sure what...) beneath their various shapes, colours and breed behaviour traits they are all basically made of the same stuff. Their visual differences do nothing to affect their basic nutritional needs as a 'dog' or the function of their bodies' different parts, such as their immune system or their digestive system.

Whilst the human intervention of 'breeding' has bred genetic visual traits and predispositional health traits to some breeds, they still all remain only a version of the 'Canis Lupus Familiaris'.

It is interesting to note that we are often quick to assess our dog's behaviour and psychology for similarities to a wolf, and yet we commonly forget the dramatic physical similarities and nutritional needs.

This book explains what types of foods the canis lupus familiaris – i.e. your dog, will thrive happily and healthily on, how a dogs digestive system actually works and answers all the most common questions and uncertainties dog owners face when choosing the best way to feed their dogs.

For us to fully understand what foods are best for our dogs we have to first consider their physical requirements and take a look at where the food goes into once it has been eaten!

No matter what it is that goes into your dog's bowl and is 'wolfed' down (couldn't resist the pun there), once in your dog's body it will all gradually get broken down, broken down and even further broken down to finally end up as simply a whole host of strings of chemicals, that pass round the dogs body doing important jobs. For instance: building cell walls, helping the liver function as a liver or switching on and off hormones.

Now we're not talking chemicals such as bleach or the liquid chemicals that immediately spring to mind from that phrase, but basically chemical elements: the ones found on the periodic table. Nutrients are chemicals and your dog's body is in fact a chemical powerhouse, working silently (at least most of the time..) to keep your dog's body alive, immune to disease and to mend it if the need to do so arises.

Just like us humans the canis familiaris has evolved to function on certain nutrients and not on others. Therefore it's quite simple to work out what to feed your dog on – find out the nutrients, and anything else that may be required, to provide exactly what their bodies need to keep them healthy, vibrant and full of balanced energy!

Dog Biology

Evolution being as clever as it is, your dog's body has not only evolved to benefit from certain nutrients but it has cleverly evolved to be physically able to digest, i.e. break down for use, these nutrients from certain food sources. It is also cleverly able to recognize **both** valuable nutrients and invaluable ones at a cellular level, it has evolved to benefit from, and require a whole host of enzymes and micro- nutrients to assist in doing so.

The next few pages aim to show what happens to your dog's food on its digestive journey. All the way from being eaten from the bowl right through to being a series of useful chemical nutrients.

A simple diagram showing the position of the organs and systems that will be mentioned throughout the book.

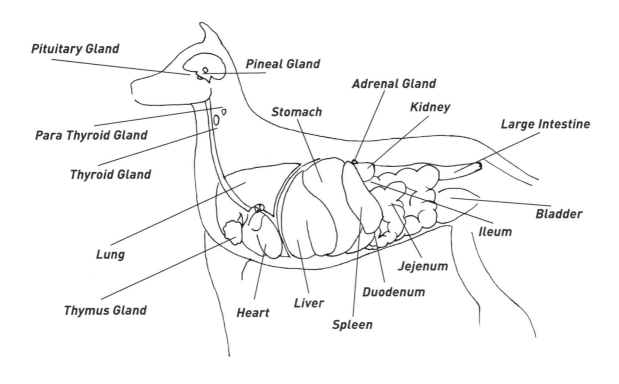

**First of all your dog gobbles up his food...
The process of breaking down food for nutrients,
begins in the mouth.**

<u>Saliva</u> : Your dog's saliva plays an entirely different role to the saliva us humans produce. There are no digestive enzymes in dog saliva. A dog's saliva is produced from 6 glands, (no. 1-6) mainly as lubrication for the bits of food that will pass down the dogs Oesophagus. It is 99% water and also plays an important role in cooling a dog down.

There is no Amylase in your dog's saliva. (Amylase: starch digesting enzyme) The dog has cleverly evolved not to produce amylase in order to protect his teeth from decay. If amylase was present starches (carbs) would be broken down into sugars and could cause dental decay. Any carbohydrate based, or sugary, treats we give our dogs will begin to undo the good this clever protective arrangement does, and could create dental issues.

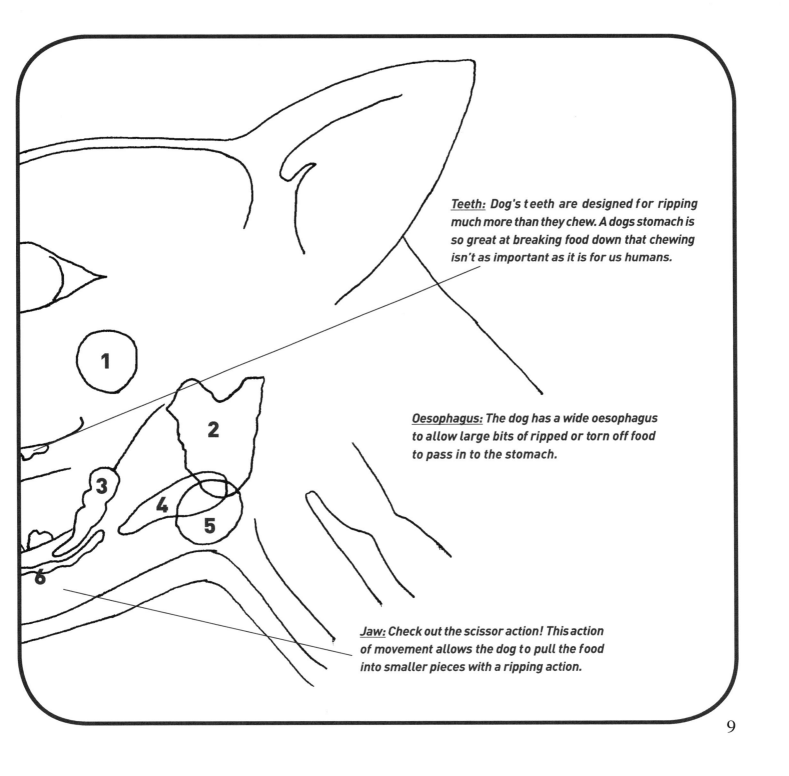

Teeth: *Dog's teeth are designed for ripping much more than they chew. A dogs stomach is so great at breaking food down that chewing isn't as important as it is for us humans.*

Oesophagus: *The dog has a wide oesophagus to allow large bits of ripped or torn off food to pass in to the stomach.*

Jaw: *Check out the scissor action! This action of movement allows the dog to pull the food into smaller pieces with a ripping action.*

1

2

3

4

5

6

The ripped up food, then passes down the oesophagus and into the stomach, which for a dog is the primary section where digestion occurs. The dogs stomach plays the primary role in digesting food, much more than their intestines do, which is the opposite to humans whose intestines do most of the work for us. Food stays in here for around 4-8hrs, in humans it stays in the stomach only about half an hour.

Stomach mucosa: Lining the stomach walls is also a layer of protective mucus. This acts to protect the stomach cells and trap bacteria. It is influenced by and could be damaged by the amount of salt found in your dog's food. Too much salt can cause the mucosa lining to decrease, leaving the stomach open to dis-ease. Most pre made dog foods state 'no added salt' - but can in fact be quite salty to begin with!

Gastrin: this gets released from glands in cells of the dogs stomach walls, when the stomach is expanded. Gastrin activates the release of more hydrochloric acid and stimulates the folds in stomach cell walls to expand and contract, churning and almost chewing away at the food inside it! The stomach will rarely expand properly on a grain based meal.

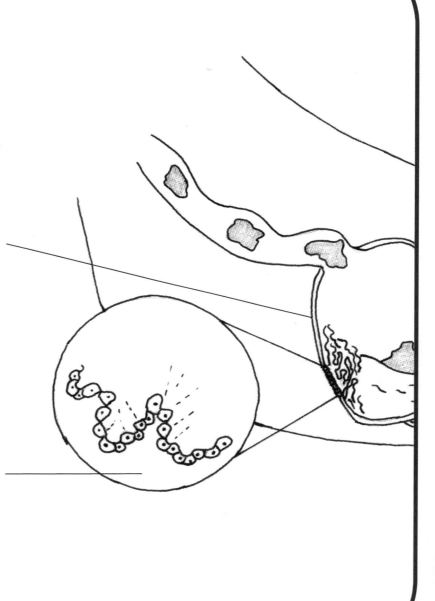

A dog is designed to eat a lot of food in one go, maybe once a day, eating until he is full and then resting. To aid with this, folds in the dogs stomach lining are cleverly able to expand to maximise the surface area of the digestive process.

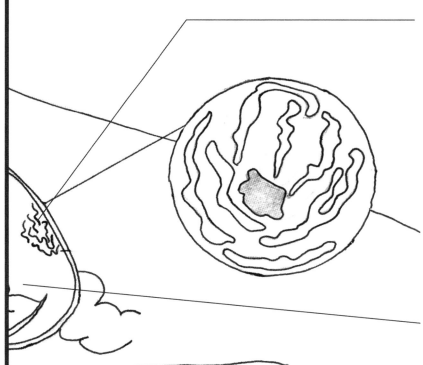

The folds found in the lining expand as the stomach becomes fuller, cleverly prompting the release of extra digestive enzymes such as gastrin and Hydrochloric acid that are needed for digestion. It is designed to function optimally, and do its job of digesting food properly, only when it is fully expanded, and these enzymes can be released.

A high ph. Balance of ph 1-2 and lots of Hydrochloric acid in there! Having a higher ph than us humans means dogs are capable of digesting bone and raw meat. The higher ph is also fabulous at killing off some of the unwanted bacteria that is live in raw meat. Unfortunately the higher ph does mean that Amylase the starch digesting enzyme does not survive well and is very rarely available for the dog, should he eat any grain or potato based food.

All these functions are the optimum way a dog digests his food to stay healthy. They apply to raw meat based diets but are compromised by grain/starch based foods

A note on Amylase and Bloat

Amylase is the digestive enzyme needed to digest starchy carbohydrates. Not only is it not present in the dog's saliva, but it does not survive well in the dog's high stomach ph level. When a dog's stomach becomes full of carbohydrate based foods, the foods are prone to staying undigested in the stomach due to a lack of this enzyme. The undigested food then stagnates, causing gasses and leaving the dogs stomach less able to expand properly, flexibly contract its cell walls and produce enough enzymes to cope with even any protein or meat based food that it does receive. Should this issue become a regular occurrence the dog begins to miss out on vital nutrients for health through the compromised digestive capabilities. In some cases it can lead to the life threatening condition called Bloat.

The whole process is worsened by starchy carbohydrates of low moisture, which are even harder for the dog's stomach to cope with.

Amylase thrives well in a ph level of 3/4 which is what we have, and is why we humans are much better able to digest starches, grains and carbohydrates!

There is a small amount of Amylase produced by the dogs pancreas. This is passed into the blood stream and can enter the 1st section of the small intestine called the Duodenum. The dogs pancreas has evolved to pass a small amount of the Amylase enzyme into the duodenum, in order for the dog to be able to cope with any starch based foods (such as grasses, plant matter or seeds) that may already be inside the gut of the prey animals that it consumes.

This small amount of starchy carbohydrate will be what the prey animal has eaten himself, prior to being killed for food. It will also have been usefully already partially digested by the prey animal before it reaches the dog's intestines and so much easier for the dog to utilize.

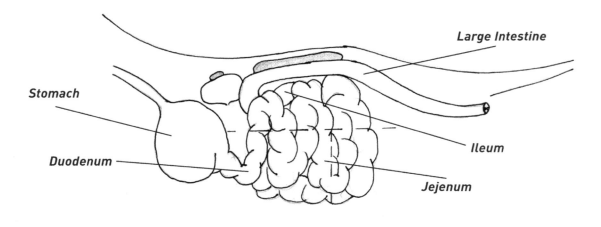

12

From the stomach the food then reaches the Duodenum

<u>Duodenum</u>: the first section of the small intestine. This is where the food passes into directly from the stomach; by now the food is already largely a great soup like mass of chemical structures, otherwise known as Nutrients!

<u>The pancreas</u> is attached here and secretes special digestive enzymes into the duodenum to assist in digesting any foods the stomach didn't deal with. It also sends its own special antibiotic secretions known as De fensins to help protect the small intestine's immunity. The enzymes from the pancreas are specially designed to help process proteins, they find it ha d to deal with carbohydrate based nutrients and can bec ome overworked if lots of those type of nutrients pass through the duodenum.

<u>The liver</u> is also abl e to pass bile through to this part of the dog's small intestine via the gall bladder. This bile also helps break down the food into nutrient molecules, it is especially good at breaking down any fatty substances.

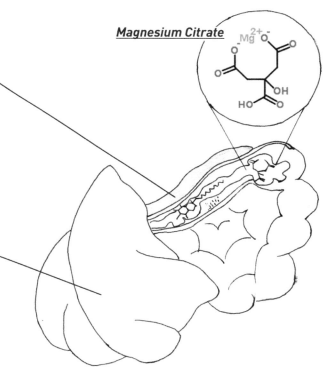

Magnesium Citrate

Hormones messages that are part of your dog's Endocrine system can directly influen e the functioning of the dog's whol e digestive system and the small in testine in particular. Hormones secreted from the adrenals, the pituitary gland and the pineal glands will influene the efficiency of the cells that make up the small intestine. Hormones are like messages to and from different body parts and organs instructing on actions to take or simply to let cells know the state of other sections of the body. If one part of the body is out of balance it can have a knock-on effect on the rest of the body and its cells.

13

Once passed through the duodenum, the food - now broken down into chemical molecules even further, goes through into the second phase of the small intestine the Jejenum. This section is lined with lots of little hair like structures called Villi which are designed to capture passing nutrients and electrolytes to make them available to the dog's cells for use.

The villi have a fantastic system of renewal which ensures they stay healthy, able to absorb nutrients and perform their other important duties in the intestine. Amongst them are lots of 'good' essential bacteria which also live on the intestinal lining. The bacteria ensure the villi renewal process takes place. The process is compromised if the intestines become sterile from drugs, such as anti-biotics, or if an overgrowth of 'bad' bacteria in the intestines occurs.

<u>Partially broken down nutrient</u> – the dog's body has a great way of detecting something it doesn't recognise, 'The immune system'. When faced with these strange looking unusable molecules/nutrients the body recognises them as problems and begins the process of removing them from the body's systems by putting them on 'alert'! It is these 'on alert' molecules that can lead to inflammatory diseases, immune reactions and allergies.

When the dog's small intestine has lots of protein based nutrients passing through it the good bacteria flourish and stay present. If this part of the intestine receives either larger, only partially digested, nutrient molecules, refined sugar molecules or molecules that result from starches having turned stagnant in the stomach as they were not fully digested. The 'good' bacteria then finds the environment unsuitable for breeding and will start to diminish.

Three main events then occur –

1. The dogs mis ses out on vital nutrien ts being passed into the blood stream for use by the body,

2. Un needed 'bad' bact eria begins to flouris instead, as the en vironment becomes perfect for them to multiply in place of the beneficial bacteria. This then compromises food absorption and nutrient assimilation which the villi and the good bacteria are there to facilitate.

3. The villi and the cell wall of the jejenum start to become weak and pr one to damage without their protective good bacteria – allowing both unwelcome bacteria, the unwelcome bacteria's toxic waste (known as endo-t oxins) and partially broken down nutrients to pass into the blood stream causing immunological reactions or dis-ease.

The Ileum the 3rd section of the small intestine, also plays an important role in digesting nutrients and even creating some too. As the food comes through from its time in the jejenum having been further broken down and some of it utilised, it then gets even further broken down in this last and 3rd part of the dog's small intestine. This final Ileum processing is all about making sure the food is fully prepared to enter the large intestine.

Once into the Large intestine the function of the large intestine is to absorb any left-over nutrients into the blood stream, as well as any water, which is vitally needed by the body too. Leaving only the waste and unneeded toxins from the food molecules, to be passed as just that - waste.

In order to do those jobs the Large Intestine maintains a level of movement in its cell walls to move the molecules around and push them further down the tube-like shape that it is. Without this movement known as peristalsis, constipation can occur.

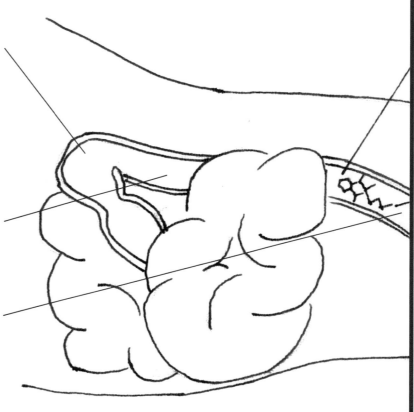

To perform peristalsis the large intestine relies on both water being available in the molecules passing through it and a good amount of the right fatty acids. These come from healthy fats which would have been earlier absorbed into the blood stream for use by the cells of the Large intestine, or still present in the food molecules as they pass through. The Large intestine can be low on fatty acids if either the useful fats were not present in the food the dog ate or if the liver and bile were compromised and unable to perform efficie tly.

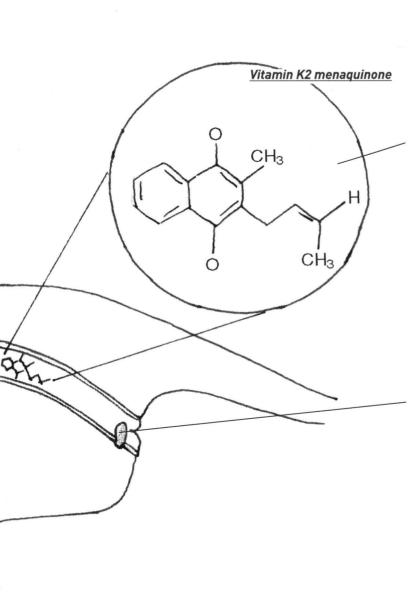

Vitamin K2 menaquinone

A healthy large intestine also plays a role in absorbing vitamins that are partly created by the intestinal bacteria, such as Vitamin B12 c obalamin, Vitamin K2 men - quinone, B1 thiamin and B2 riboflvin. It also relies on a healthy flexible cellular wall in order to absorb nutrients optimally.

<u>Anal Glands</u> - a raw diet can be really useful for dogs that have anal gland issues. Due to the bone content the waste passed from a raw diet is much firmer than waste passed from a processed dog food diet. The firmne s naturally expresses the anal glands of the dog as it passes. Meaning trips to the vet or expressing them yourself can be a thing of the past, and your dog will definitely feel more contented.

The importance of the Liver and its influence on digestion.

As well as sending and creating bile via the **gall** bladder to the 1st portion of the small **intestine** the liver also helps to produce extra **energy** for your dog from stores of glycogen. The **energy** is created as a reaction whilst the liver does its work of clearing out stored, potentially harmful, toxins or chemicals from the dogs body.

For this process to happen the liver needs to be able to recognise the energy is needed. If a dog's stomach and intestines are constantly being filled to a minimum level - for example if food is left down for the dog to nibble or graze on throughout the day, or if food is stagnating and undigested in the stomach or intestines - the liver is not sent the signals in order to recognise and produce energy from its glycogen stores as often.

When a dog's stomach and intestines are constantly being filled or topped up to a minimum level, a higher than usual amount of glycogen or sugars, will get released into the blood stream from all that food as it passes into the small intestine. The dog's body will begin to turn to those sugars for its energy and the liver can then simply put its feet up with a cup of tea... Which is great for all the lazy livers out there, but not so great for the rest of your dog as they simply become full of toxins, less able to produce energy from the liver stores if they do need it and become the kind of dog that is always seeking out food as a top up for their energy levels and unsatisfied gut system.

Furthermore the then somewhat sluggish liver is less able to perform its other vital functions:

like thyroid hormone conversion for instance, regulating pituitary gland function, or as mentioned before, creating bile to help digest essential fatty acids from food in the small intestine.

Text books seem to differ slightly, but it takes approximately between 12-18 hours for the dog's gut system to fully digest a raw dinner and become empty again. It is at this point the dog's body turns to the liver for its energy. This is the stage that allows the liver to function and do its amazing jobs. Jobs that your dog cannot survive healthily without!

The irony is that a dog fed either on starch based foods **or** sometimes even on cooked meats will often appear very hungry and constantly looking for food. Firstly he may well have become physically reliant on energy from the food in the stomach and intestine, or at least his systems will react as if he has until they get the chance to recognise the liver's role again, and secondly the foods will be creating his blood to be in an acid state, as opposed to a healthy alkaline state, which in turn creates cravings for more acid forming foods.

We may easily be led to feel we are caring **for** them **better by allowing them to eat more and** yet in **reality we are creating hunger in an animal we are attempting to nourish and satisfy.**

Enzymes and the Acid, Alkali Balance

One of the main aims of the foods included in a raw diet, as well as fulfilling the dogs nutritional requirements, is that the diet will keep the dog's blood, lymph and tissue functioning in an **alkaline** state.

In order to keep the dog's stomach at a high acidic PH, the cells around the stomach need to be able to recognize the rest of the body as **alkaline**. They form a sort of guide for the stomach's cells to know how acid it needs to be. If feedback shows the body to be acidic, the stomach is not encouraged to produce as high a PH level, and when the dog is in a healthy alkali state the stomach is fed back the information and will recognize its need to be just the opposite. The pancreas also functions better while the body is in an **alkaline** state, releasing stronger amounts of its digestive enzymes and even certain enzymes which are reported to play a role in destroying cancer cell barriers.

When the dog's body is in an acid state he will be more susceptible to infections, general aches and pains, may put on weight and feel stressed or fatigued more frequently. The acid state body fluids will also compromise the dog's skeletal system by leaching minerals from **areas such as** bones in order to correct the acid/alkali balance, thus weakening bones,skin, fur and nails. A dog in an acid state will show cravings for more acid foods and may feel hungry more often.

Another attribute of raw foods is their volume of enzymes. Enzymes are very easily destroyed by cooking and processing of foods and yet they are fundamental to the digestive process and also to keeping the cells of the body metabolising and regenerating. No doubt nutrients alone could keep a body alive but it is these enzymes that keep a body alive, full of vitality and health. They are used by the body to digest nutrients, and as catalysts to many of the chemical reactions that need to occur for optimum health.

Many of these reactions are oxygen related reactions, where by the molecules in the food lose and acquire electrons in an energy exchange to encourage healing and regeneration. Cooking destroys oxygen containing enzymes and many nutrients such as Vitamin C, which have similar actions.

Cells of living creatures are known to have something called antagonistic micro-electrical tensions. This process is one of the ways that cells of the body communicate with each other and also one of the ways they are able to attract needed nutrients and reject those that are unneeded or harmful. It is an interchange of energy between the cells and the capillaries of the blood stream.

Studies in Vienna have shown that raw foods increase this micro-electrical tension. This Means that the cells and capillaries are better able to carry nutrients in or out of cells, and importantly to carry harmful substances away from cells to be detoxed from the body. If a diet of cooked foods is a constant, the membranes between the cells and the capillaries can gradually build up with waste products and ultimately lead to cellular degeneration and aging.

Some conclusions so far..

You have now seen for yourself how the dog's digestive system, and the organs related to it, all function. I hope it is now much clearer to you why they are able to cope with certain foods and not others. You can also understand what happens when their bodies do try to digest the foods they are not designed to deal with. Doesn't it just make so much more sense when you can see the scientific why's and how's!

Just to recap and mention a few of the most important facts:

It is worth mentioning that each dog is an individual and will be born with individual cellular well-being levels. Perhaps with a predisposition to a weakness in certain organs or whole systems. After all they are only a product of their parents' own cellular systems, genetic predispositions and nutrient levels. A lack of nutrients or compromised body systems will show up in a different way for every dog, producing a whole host of various symptoms or disease.

All sections of the dog's body work holistically, one part influences the other and all cells communicate constantly – the health of the dog as a whole has a far greater influence than attempting to cure symptoms of individual organs or body parts.

By not having starch digestive enzymes **present** in their saliva, a dog protects his teeth from decay. Adding grain/starch based treats to the diet upsets this useful attribute.

Grain based foods compromise the function of the teeth, the stomach, the stomach lining, the small intestine, the nutrient absorbing villi, the flexibility of the colon walls and the liver's metabolism. They contain very little useful nutrients for a dog.

An imbalance of intestinal bacteria or an overgrowth of 'bad' bacteria can lead to something called Gut Dysbiosis, which is damage to the intestinal wall. This can allow larger undigested molecules to pass into the dogs blood stream leading to intolerances and allergies. Candida and other unwanted bacteria feed on nutrients and sugars from grain based foods. They survive well and multiply easily in the environments such food creates in the dog's digestive system.

The liver's function is compromised by a grain based diet and also by a constant or too regular supply of food into the stomach and small intestine.

The correct fatty acids are imperative to the function of the dog's digestive system, in fact every cell in his body. Biologically Fats are one of your dog's primary energy sources.

Enzymes are hugely influential and one of the bodies most missed elements in a cooked diet.

'' To eat is a necessity,
   to eat intelligently is an art''
   – Francois de la Rochefouchaud. author

21

Fats, and the possibility of Feeding cooked meat and vegetables instead of raw meat

We can see from the explanation of the function of the dog's gut systems and digestive abilities that meat foods are better for them. But how about feeding those exact same foods, only cooked instead of raw?

Any cooking that you do at home will have an effect on the food and it will reduce the availability of nutrients and enzymes your dog could get from his diet. Heat and light changes the chemical structure of food and its nutrients.

Heated protein is vastly different from raw protein, and the higher the temperature the greater the structure gets altered. A dog is biologically designed to function on as pure a protein as possible, one that is unchanged by heat. There are a variety of enzymes found in food that are needed by the dog's gut system for digestion. These will be affected at temperatures of 110f and more. This temperature breaks the molecular bond of the enzymes, making them unavailable and challenging food digestion. There are also some vitamins and minerals that are destroyed by heat and light, this too will have an effect on your dog's health as vitamins and minerals are essential to the dogs ability to use nutrients to perform tasks like building bones, making new cells, liver function and hormone regulation and all the other internal functions of his/her body.

By far the most influential change that occurs during a cooking process though, is the change to the structure of fats and the important essential fatty acids that are found in dietary fats. Dogs are not designed to utilise glucose from carbohydrates as a primary source of energy. A dog's body take its energy source from oxidizing appropriate proteins and from certain types of fats. The energy is used for movement, for cellular respiration, for brain activity and the general functioning of the all parts and cells of the dogs body. Which makes it vital that the correct proteins, enzymes, fats and fatty acids are available in their diet.

Fats are hugely unstable in heat and even in light. Their structures are very easily altered during any cooking process. Most of you will have heard of the term 'omega 3', it has even become quite a buzz word. However questioning the level of omega 3 in a diet is just the start of an understanding into the value of fats in the diet.

Fatty acids come in 2 main types. Cis-Fatty Acids which are the natural form, recognized by the dog's cells, and Trans-Fatty Acids which are created when exposed to heat, light and oxygen. Cis-Fatty Acids are converted by the dog's body into useful and usable hormones which protect cell walls, keeping them flexible, in order to let nutrients pass in and toxins to pass out of the cell. As well as protecting from invading viruses or bacteria, they also very importantly regulate the 'inflammatory' and 'anti-inflammatory' reactions your dog will have within his body. Trans Fatty Acids are not recognized by the dogs cells and are toxins. They form fatty deposits in the dog's body and in its blood vessel walls. They allow for the cell walls to become inflexible and susceptible to viruses, bacteria and an imbalance of nutrients. They also crucially compete for space within the hormone conversion pathways that regulate the dog's inflammatory and anti-inflammatory reactions. Meaning dogs are left susceptible to inflammatory 'allergic' reactions to internal or external toxins, and are unable to self regulate inflammation caused during injury or joint wear and tear.

It has become common for pre-made dog food companies to spray the foods with fatty acids oils in an effort to restore the essential fatty acids dogs need. This is often either done prior to cooking though and thus means the subsequent heat destroys them again or the fats sprayed are from heat extracted sources to begin with. The damage and imbalance that the carbohydrates, heated proteins and resulting trans fatty acids do to the dog's digestive and cellular systems means that any left over EFA's are unable to create their conversion pathways. They are also left with little nutrients to assist them in their conversion to the useful hormones.

CIS fatty acids Follow various pathways meeting nutrients along the way, to create Prostagladin Hormones

Omega 6
Linolenic Acid

Converts to GLA then creates

Omega 3
Alpha Linoleic Acid

Converts to EPA then creates

Omega 6 Pathways are blocked by Sugar, Stress, Trans fatty acids, Refined Flours, Excess Mono-unsaturated & Mono-saturated fats, lack of certain vitamins and minerals.

Omega 3 Pathways only exist when the fats are included in the diet.

Prostagladin Hormones

P H 1 Anti-Inflammatory and when meets Arachondric acid creates PG2 Inflammatory

P H 3 and PH 12 Anti-Inflammatories Also cancels out excess PG2 created from high arachondric acid levels.

TRANS fatty acids
Compete with Omega 6 and 3 to take up space in the various pathways.

PH 1, P H 3 and PH 12 Anti-Inflammatories are not created. Also any excess PG2 Inflammatory, created from high arachondric acid levels in the diet, does not get cancelled out as easily.

With the understanding of this information, it is easy for us to see why it is that more dogs are being diagnosed with inflammatory diseases such as arthritis, dermatitis and even cancer. By providing your dog with food that can be broken down into useful fatty acids and nutrients that his body can use to stay healthy, you will be providing your dog with a far higher chance to thrive and stay healthy, even into old age.

Balanced Diet

"Our philosophy is not best
expressed in words;
it is expressed in the choices
we make... and the choices
we make are ultimately our
responsibility"
– *Eleanor Roosevelt*

24

I would at this point like to encourage you to do a lot more research into feeding your dog a raw diet. Now you can see how the dog's body functions, and just how imperative raw food is for dogs, you will now be much better placed to understand the types of foods and volumes to feed your own dogs, as individuals.

These are a few basic food options that you can consider for your dog. Now I have empowered you with the knowledge of why raw works best for them, I hope you will enjoy researching more into raw feeding your dogs and watching them grow and develop, into healthy balanced canine friends.

Food options to consider

Meats: Game meats tend to be better for dogs than farm meats. Choose from; Rabbit, Pheasant, Deer, Chicken, Turkey, Lamb, Beef, Goat, Elk, even Kangaroo - if you are in the right country!

Meats both on and off the bone are fantastic, whole carcasses will be relished. These are great at keeping your dog's teeth nice and clean too. Organ meats/Offal are a fantastic way to provide nutrients. Try to include offal sometimes too, such as heart, lung, liver. Be aware that these meats are quite rich so start with smaller amounts. Green Tripe is useful to consider as it contains a valuable amount of enzymes, positive bacteria and amino acids. Source yourself some that has been washed to ensure it is safe for human handling. Dogs can also benefit hugely from and enjoy fish, including the bones, when given raw. Fish such as, sardines or mackerel will be a fantastic source of the essential omega fatty acids.

Vegetables- preferably liquidized, grated or minced: An easy way to get the balance right is to include one type of above ground veggie and one variety of below ground veggie. So for instance carrot, which grows below ground, could be put with spinach or broccoli, which grow above ground.

Additions: Live sheep or goats yoghurt is a great addition. This will be lapped up by most dogs and could promote beneficial gut bacteria.

Also by including herbs such as Parsley, Kelp or Alfalfa you will be ensuring that your dog benefits from a full spectrum of vitamins and minerals on a daily basis. Eggs can also be included, organic eggs are particularly useful as they contain higher levels of essential omega fatty acids than free range eggs. Battery hen eggs are unlikely to contain very much of the fatty acids at all. The crushed shells of eggs can add valuable minerals to the dog's diet.

Meaty Bones : These are a staple part of feeding a raw diet to your dog. Avoid bones that are harder than your dogs teeth, puppies will have weaker teeth than adult dogs. A larger knucklebone is a good starter bone for adult dogs who have not had bones before. Start with softer bones from young animals and move on to the harder weight bearing joint bones as the dog becomes used to bones. Feeding raw poultry carcasses is a great way to include both the meat and meaty bones in one meal.

Feeding Salmon: Dogs do benefit from eating the essential fatty acids and protein types in salmon. However there have been reports of dogs suffering as a result of eating raw salmon contaminated with a bacteria called Neorickettsia helminthoeca. It may be wise to lightly cook your dogs salmon to destroy the bacteria.

Supplements and vitamin tablets

A dog fed on a healthy variety based raw diet shouldn't need much in the way of supplements. The correct nutrients should be available in the food itself. However from time to time, perhaps during a period of illness or if you are converting your dog to raw food after a time eating pre-made dog food. Then you may want to include an additional immune boosting probiotic supplement or supplement of the essential fatty acids (the omegas).

There are some probiotics on the market that are designed and manufactured specifically for dogs These are worth looking into. Currently only one type of probiotic bacteria is used in veterinary supplements but the commercial varieties contain a much broader spectrum and at least begin to recognise the value of including multi strains of probiotic bacteria.

Essential omega 3 fatty acids are best given as a fish oil rather than the flaxseed oils which **are** popular for humans. Although flax is usable by dogs, fatty acids from fish oil are far easier for them to utilise. Fish oils are best given as multi fish oils often labelled as EPA supplements, as opposed to simply cod liver oil on its own. Cod liver oil contains far less Omega 3, which is the aim of the supplementation, and also could lead to an overdose of Vitamin A if given regularly.

Dependant on your dog as an individual, including his history of diet and well-being issues, you may also wish to supplement his diet with omega 6 fatty acids too. These are most easily found in supplements of Evening primrose oil. Always buy fatty acids supplements as Cold Pressed, Organic and from shops that keep the supplement tubs or bottles away from heat and light sources.

Supplements of green superfood plants such as Spirulina and chlorella could also be of use, especially at times of illness or when you are changing your dog over to his new diet. I have clients who swear that including chlorella in their dogs diet works as breath freshener for him. If the breath is fresh then it is a sure sign the gut system is also fresh too! Spirulina is also packed with pure protein amino acids and contains the essential fatty acids.

These kinds of supplements contain a range of nutrients in very natural forms, which means your dog's body can take just as much of the nutrients it needs, and easily secrete the rest. This makes them a much safer supplement to add, rather than trying to supplement your dog with individual nutrients that you have read somewhere may be useful for certain situations or well-being issues.

How much to give

The general rule in the pet food sector, is that your dog should have around 2% - 3% of its body weight per day. So it is definitely worth getting your dog weighed so you know where to start. Just as with yourself and your family, the best way to know if your dog individually needs a bit more, or even a bit less than the 2% a day is to keep an eye on his physical body, activity levels and behaviour. Most dogs I know personally, that are fed on the raw meaty bones diet are actually fed around 1% or 1.5% of their body weight and thrive very well. The general rule could well be from a ratio of dogs on pre-made dog food.

A calculation that is commonly used to work out how many calories your dog will need on a daily basis is: 2 x (30 x 'weight of dog in kg') + 70 ='s ' calories needed a day'. Obviously if your dog is particularly active he or she may need more. But again this will change on a daily basis so the best thing you can do is keep an eye on his physical body, activity levels and behaviour yourself and adjust accordingly. As with all diets, puppies and pregnant bitches will need more food. I have included a Puppy Feeding chart at the back of the book as a guideline.

As an example I might give my West Highland Terrier X a couple of poultry drumsticks or wings a day plus some goats yoghurt with a sprinkling of ground flaxseed and home grown parsley. Or perhaps a big handful of green tripe plus liquidised greens. This is in addition to her chewing at her bone off and on during the day from which she will be obtaining nutrients from also.

A friend of mine with large Husky X GSD's might give them each per day - 1 turkey thigh, 200g ox liver, plus pulsed vegetables or 4 chicken carcasses each, plus a lambs heart, and pulsed fruit & veg. She also likes to give her dogs egg, cottage cheese, live yogurt, extra virgin olive oil, cold pressed linseed oil, & garlic.

Some advocates of raw feeding recommend feeding only raw meat and meaty bones, without supplements or vegetables. Others recommend a diet with raw meat, meaty bones plus vegetables and additions, such as live yoghurt. **The best thing to do is work out what is right for your dog as an individual.** Consider your dogs diet history. For instance, dogs that have been fed processed food for a while may benefit from additions and vegetables for the extra nutrients.

I always do my best to find organic meat for my dog. This can be more expensive, but avoids any residual toxins from the growth hormones or chemicals the animals in an intensive farming environment may have been given.

Although you can never be 100% sure that you are feeding a completely pure toxin free diet. Feeding a raw diet is so much more immune building that it is much less likely your dog would actually be harmed by any stray toxins from the chemical biased environment us humans are creating here on planet earth.

For those of you who really don't want to make the food up yourself there are now several companies who make raw food meals up and will deliver it to you.

5/10% grain concept

If you happen to have: an active working dog, a dog that regularly takes part in canine sports such as agility or fly-ball, a fast growing young puppy or perhaps a large breed dog who perhaps is finding that obtaining his required energy levels from a totally raw meaty bones based diet is challenging at first. Then you'll be pleased to hear that there is a general talked about 'rule' that including about 5% of high moisture grains in the diet plan could be of benefit to these types of dogs while they are making the transition to a raw diet.

The key though is to include grains that have a good moisture content, and that have had as little processing as possible, wholegrain is best!

Options could include wheat germ, rice bran husks or soaked oat bran.

Commercial dog food, even wholegrain biscuit meal has a much lower moisture content but if that is used it's best to stick at a lower %, around 3%, which does on a practical level make it almost pointless to include, but if it is all you can obtain it will have to do until their transition is complete.

Absolute no no's

Please avoid the following food stuffs, as they contain substances poisonous to a canis lupus familiaris: Grapes, Raisins, Chocolate, Rhubarb, Onion, **Coffee,** Apple pips, Macadamia Nuts, Walnuts – or any fruit stone.

Try to use Garlic only when it may be beneficial medicinally as an anti-parasite herb, sticking to wild **garlic** whenever possible.
Never feed cooked bones!!

Meaty Bones

If you do one thing after reading this book I hope it will be this: Enjoy watching your dog's delight and gratitude at being able to chew away at a raw bone.

The act of chewing on a bone encourages a great natural plaque clearing, teeth cleaning action for your dog. Bones also contain an amazing array of nutrients readily available for your dog's cells and systems.

I'm sure we can all agree on Calcium but just look at the whole host of others too!

Raw meaty bones are a staple part of a dog being fed a Raw diet. Should you choose to purchase packaged raw food meals be sure to also include bones in the dog's diet, both for the nutritional benefits and importantly, the behavioural considerations.

The benefits of chewing are widely known as relaxing and confidence boosting. Endorphins are released when dogs chew, travelling round the body and counteracting stress hormones. Endorphins are part of the dog's Limbic system, which is hugely involved in the formation of their memories and emotions. The mouth area itself is linked with the Limbic system and is often referred to as the 'seat of emotions'. Chewing on bones will also help your dog to release any built up stress or tension in his jaw and mouth area. In that way also influencing how he feels and behaves on a daily basis.

What's in bones?

Calcium, Iron
Magnesuim
Manganese
Boron, Phosphorous
Vitamin K2
Glucosamine
'Essential Fatty Acids
(Omega's)'
Anti-oxidants
Vitamins A, D, E
'Unaltered Amino
Acids'
Valuable Enzymes

Common Concerns & Questions

"The important thing is not to stop questioning. Curiosity has its own reason for exsisting.
One cannot help but be in awe when he contemplates the mysteries of eternity, life and of the marvelous structure of reality"
– Albert Einstein

Will my dog get diarrhoea if I simply switch over to a raw diet?

Every dog is different, because their gut system will be at a different stage of growth and well being. Some dogs will benefit from simply switching straight over to raw whereas others may need a more gradual change. If you are worried about the change then do it gradually, introducing more raw ingredients to his food bowl over the course of a week or so, letting them become used to digesting it.

It is more common for older dogs or dogs that have had a previous unhealthy diet to be less able to digest a new raw diet. This is because over time their gut system will have become a little redundant on the enzyme and digestion front, and like all parts of a physical body, if something is not used it becomes dormant or simply not at optimum. The wrong kind of foods entering the body can also influence a lack of production of the enzymes. With the right nutrients and care of the gut system these enzymes can return though, all is not lost!

The main thing is that, if your dog simply has a slightly looser stool, don't panic! This may well be his body getting used to the new food and passing out any toxins from the previous food types. If it persists, or if his demeanour changes, or if it contains blood or if you are worried, then do see a vet.

Will my dog choke on bones?

Cooked bones should not be fed for this very reason, especially smaller brittle bones, such as poultry bones. Raw uncooked bones are much more flexible and digestible. As with all foods and treats and even chewing of your slippers to be honest, there is a risk of choking. Have you witnessed the speed some dogs eat dry premade dog food? It's a wonder there is not more choking on dry food too!
The benefits to the dog of eating a raw diet completely outweigh any of our personal fears of them choking on bones, especially when they are fed sensibly and if need be, kept an eye on.

I'm sure most wolves standing over the carcass of their dinner do not remind each other to be careful of choking! Yet having said that, it is always useful to keep an eye on your dog if he is eating bones as part of a meal as opposed to chewing outside of dinner time. Certain bones such as vertebrae bones can be small enough to get stuck in the dog's **oesphagus** if they eat them too quickly.

It is worth avoiding feeding bones that are harder than your dog's teeth. Teeth too can be prone to damage and if your dog has been fed a pre made dog food for a while, they may not be in tip top condition either, leaving them more prone to damage. In general bones from the weight bearing joints of an animal are harder than bones from the neck for instance. Try starting off with the softer raw bones from poultry or smaller lamb bones.

Why hasn't my vet told me about this?

Believe it or not there **is** a growing number of vets **who** actually recommend feeding a raw diet. Sensible vets tend to steer clear of recommending anything they are not trained in or have a full understanding of, which is fantastic because you then know you can trust them for their total honesty.

However there is a huge (and growing) number of vets worldwide who are now recommending and learning about the benefits of raw feeding. Excitingly many are also rediscovering their interest in researching the sciences behind the dog's gut system biology. After all biology and chemistry is what vets base their knowledge on.

Historically the only diet and nutrition based education that most vets have had , has been funded by the companies that manufacture pre-made dog food.

Therefore their education has been primarily focused on the content of these foods and not on the functional biology and chemistry of a dog's gut system. I understand that on average during the 6 years it takes to train as a vet an average of only six weeks are spent looking at diet. I think that unless they take a special interest in learning about the biology of dog's gut, vets simply may not have enough knowledge to recommend the diet to you in the honest way they prefer to practice.

Is Raw Feeding more expensive?

As with all products you buy, it depends on where you buy it. Be savvy! Shop around for the best deals, grab the marked down liver or kidneys from the reduced shelves in supermarkets (it is common to find them because so few people buy them these days!). Choose fish from the freezer (usually cheaper) or when it's on special deals.
Stock your freezer up if need be.

Feeding a raw diet shouldn't be any more expensive than a mid-range quality pre-made dog food, in fact it will be cheaper than the expensive brands often marketed at dogs with gut system or digestive issues! Feeding a raw diet will be more expensive than the cheap and cheerful pre-made dog food sacks but isn't your dog worth so very much more than that anyway?

It is now possible to grow your own vegetables in even the smallest of gardens (or window boxes!) and definitely easy to grow herbs such as parsley or sage.

Bones can usually be obtained from a butcher, although it is becoming tougher because many of them are restricted with health and safety laws and often have to throw the bones away rather than give you them. It's worth persevering though, as explained earlier bones are quite possibly the loveliest most caring thing you can ever provide for your dog!

There are also a number of companies now providing frozen raw food too! Most deliver so you can stock up. Some of our favourite ones are included at the end of this book.

My dog buries and digs up his bones..

What fun! So you have a happy dog... but maybe a dodgy looking lawn! Although common, not all dogs will do this. As digging is actually part of a dog's emotional instincts and release of tension, the ones that do it should be encouraged rather than discouraged. They can easily be trained to use a specific part of the garden to do their burying. Contact a friendly positive dog trainer who can help you with this if need be. Although Clicker training a command of 'go to your place' and a good dose of patience can also work wonders. Despite our human concerns over the cleanliness of the bone, your dog will often prefer it to be to grubbiest it can be, full of enzymes from the soil! If you are worried don't 'clean it' but simply blanche it in boiling water to kill off some of the 'germs' you may be worried about. The further into raw feeding you get the more your dog's gut system will have healed and be able to cope with grubby looking buried and dug up bones!

Won't there be flies around my dog's raw food?

It is not common for dogs to leave raw food in the bowl. Most can't believe their luck at finally being fed something so delicious, and that their bodies are designed to function on. Should your dog leave some of their dinner the best thing is to take it up and give it back to them later. Note also that the dogs stomach ph is much higher than ours, at 1-2ph and is thus far more capable to destroying most **bacteria**.

My dog doesn't seem to know what this Raw food is! Could I warm it up or perhaps heat-seal the meat in a frying pan?

Some dogs are led by a higher scent drive than others when it comes to their food. These dogs seem to not be keen on eating cold, bland smelling food. In these cases I would recommend firstly taking the food out of the fridge and letting it reach room temperature before feeding it to your dog. (Don't forget to cover it to protect from flies or, other hungry creatures, while doing so!)

Secondly you could even try cutting into the meat and letting the juices run through for them to smell. Also rubbing interesting smelling herbs onto the meats or rubbing a little garlic may make a difference and help the food smell more appealing to .such dogs. (check any herbs used are suitable for dogs!)

Please do also refer to the section on feeding home cooked food for more information about heating your dogs dinner.

Why does my pre-made dog food packaging say it is 'Complete' or indicate it contains all the nutrients my dog needs?

This is a question I too raised when I first began to learn about the foods that a dog is biologically designed to eat. I knew that the labelling laws for human food were constantly being checked for authenticity and to make sure all the relevant information on ingredients and nutritional content were included. I also knew that the advertising standards agency were the organization who work to make sure that all claims either in advertising or on packaging is honest and truthful. So why was it that claims of dog food being nutritionally complete or natural were included on the pre-made cooked dog food, if that wasn't the case?

One answer lies in the fact that the labelling laws that surround dog foods are much less stringent than the human labelling laws. Dog food companies employ bright marketing staff who work out how to inventively promote dog foods to make them seem appealing to owners, and easily still keep within the minimal laws that do exist.

UK trading standards labelling laws state that all dog foods have to be classed as either complete or **complementary**. The word 'Complete' simply means that the food does not require any additional feed added to it, for instance with a pre-made dry food, and 'Complementary' means the feed does require the addition of another feed, such as with a mixer biscuit that contains no protein. It is not a statement that the food is full of all the enzymes, micro nutrients and digestible nutrients that a dog's body needs for growth and health.

It is interesting to note that the criteria a dog food has to meet to be classed as complete is only officially regulated prior to the manufacturing and cooking process. Which means that by the time the food reaches its packaging the nutrients originally present in the ingredients, will have been compromised and altered. What is going into the packet is completely structurally different to what was intended!

Very little funding is made available (at least in UK) for the regulation of pet foods after they have been manufactured. Any work done to check up on food claims puts humans first, then farm animals and pet food at the end of the list.

The original guideline of nutritional requirements set by the Association of American Feed Control Officials (AAFCO) is the general guideline used by pet food companies worldwide. It is not a complete break down of the chemical enzymatic requirements. It does not take into account dogs as individuals, or the fact that some nutrients work synergistically with others. It was also originally set to levels that are classed as the absolute minimum requirements for a dog. Yet to be classed as complete a dog food only has to contain 'some of' the essentials and not necessarily those essentials even at the minimum requirement level.

What do I feed if he/she is sick-poorly

Cooked chicken and rice seems to be the favourite wives tale if you have a poorly or under the weather dog. Sometimes it is known for owners to be recommended to completely remove protein altogether and only feed grains.

Having read and understood the function of a dogs gut system's in this book, we can see that those choices are not really the best for the dog. The aim of them is to improve the digestibility of the food given, yet in effect they would be doing the exact opposite.

A day with no food may be all your dog needs to perk up and relieve any loose stools, vomiting or bloating. If your dog is convalescing, it would be far healthier to simply reduce the amount of food your dog eats than to change it to something less digestible such as carbohydrates.

It is worth researching a good pro-biotic to add to your dog's food. There are some good makes such as whose products are aimed specifically at dogs and carry more than 1 strain of beneficial bacteria. Of course if you are worried please do visit a vet.

Should I give him/her a starvation day?

Some advocates of the raw diet do recommend having a day when you don't provide food. This is said to mimic the diet of wolves or wild dogs as sometimes days go by until their next feed. What we do know is that the liver is a majorly important organ, and it functions best when the gut system is empty – which with a raw meal can take around 12- 18hrs sometimes up to 30 for some dogs (longer with more carb/grain based foods) and so sometimes a starvation day is actually a nice thing to do for your dog's well-being and health.

However, this is entirely dependent on your dog. Only you will know how he or she is with or without

a day off. The main thing is to remember that it is not a problem if your dog doesn't want to eat for a day. Dogs know how they feel inside and instinctively avoid eating if they feel their digestion is not up to it. This is often at times of stress, a change to their environment or during a period of nervousness. The worst thing for their gut systems health is to force them to eat at these times. You might wish to try a technique such as Tellington T Touch on their mouth area to reduce nervousness, or the emotions behind the behaviour of not eating. But if they really don't eat for days it is worth visiting a vet to be certain they are ok.

Could this diet improve or influence my dog's immune system or health?

In a word, Yes! It goes without saying that a diet rich in the chemical nutrients that are usable to the recipient will improve its chances of producing the chemical reactions, hormones, molecules and cellular states it is naturally programmed to create to keep healthy.

The gut system and the mucosal lining of it are the first line of defence for your dog's immune system, screening out potentially harmful substances and toxins from reaching the blood stream.

However as we have seen, feeding a diet full of the kinds of foods can challenge or even damage this important gut lining, affecting a dog's health and well-being in lots of ways. Most cases of inflammation in a dog's body can be influenced by the state of the dogs digestive system, and also by the types of fatty acids that are present in the diet fed to them.

One of the most popular supplements on the market for dogs is Glucosamine. This is generally marketed as being great for their joints as indeed Glucosamine is involved in the creation of collagen, ligaments, cartilage and tendons. What is not often mentioned is that Glucosamine is also the amino sugar that

dogs use as a precursor to creating the fluid that coats the mucous membrane in the gut lining. It is also used to create the IGA antibody that is contained in the gut lining. With a supplementation of Glucosamine, you are not only helping your dog's joints but also his gut defences, which when healthy, will help your dogs cells to react in a less inflammatory way throughout his body. Raw meaty bones will contain plenty of Glucosamine, plus the other amino sugars and nutrients that work with it.

There are nowadays branches of science which specifically study the links between the digestive system and the immune system, and even the link between the digestive system and the function of the brain. After all chemicals are measurable 'things' and the processes of the gut are scientifically distinguishable.

In many ways the veterinary sciences are still catching up with human sciences. As the veterinary community do so, they will be better able to research, for instance, the many different strains of bacteria that may be beneficial to dogs. Plus ways to get those bacteria supplements through the dog's high PH stomach to the jejenum in order for them to be useful.

Wow.. This all sounds like feeding pre made commercial dog food is quite bad for a dog to eat. If so why do so many dogs seem to be so healthy while being fed it?!

I guess that comes down to how you define healthy! With exception of those animals who are telepathically communicated with by an animal communicator, our dogs are basically unable to tell us should they be suffering from various aches and pains, even a headache or perhaps feeling a lack of energy. Think about how you begin to feel if you eat too much, or eat lots of high fat or sugary foods. Your dog could well be feeling the same.

Unless we can see an external symptom or a major difference in our dogs energy levels it is easy to put their behaviours down to personality or dispositions. In fact behaviour issues are some of the ways that foods can affect a dog before any health issue or symptom shows. Just like us, your dog has what's called a blood brain barrier, which lets in nutrients the brain requires to regulate behaviours and thought processes. This blood brain barrier can be compromised by the larger undigested molecules your dog's body puts 'on alert'. It is also primarily dependant on the correct fatty acids which play a strong role in the health and function of the nervous systems. Dogs fed foods which compromise the nutrients that reach the brain and nervous systems are then less able to regulate their behaviour as easily as

dogs getting all the nutrients its nervous system needs, thus more likely to show 'bad' or 'reactive' behaviour labels such as highly strung, nervous, over excitability or even the often over used misunderstood label of dominance.

The change in dog feeding over the past 50 years or so could well be playing a role in the rise of behaviour issues in dogs.

Another important point to this question is that the incidence of allergic reactions and inflammatory disease in dogs, including arthritis and cancer, has risen steadily the longer that pre-made dogs foods have been available to feed, (since around the 1960's).

So on the whole it seems that dogs are not actually any healthier being fed these kinds of foods. Because dogs live a shorter life span than ourselves, it has taken a much shorter time for the effects of a non-biological or if you like, scientifically correct diet to be noticed. I personally think it is an important influential factor in the health of us humans too, and that perhaps we should consider eating a lot more raw foods ourselves too!... Although perhaps not raw meat!

Real Life Stories

Feeding a Raw Diet is one of the most responsible caring things you can do for your dog. Switching to a raw diet can dramatically change dog's lives for the better. A raw diet can not only positively influence the health and well-being of your dog, but also positively influence his behaviour too.

The next few pages are dedicated to some real life raw feeding stories and articles, you might even recognise a few of the faces ☺

Macgyver and his owner Sophi, celebrity dog trainer Sophi Stewart.

Macgyver is a glorious looking 5yr old long haired German Shepherd with lush coat, bright eyes and incredibly calm, sought after disposition. He enjoys a dream canine life assisting his owner to train dogs, care for dogs while their owners are on holiday and join dogs on inspiring walks in some of London's finest parklands. He even enjoyed a promising career as a hospital PAT dog, cheering up poorly children and the elderly alike. Yet up until a year ago poor Macgyver's life was tainted by a rare auto immune disease that can affect large breed dogs, a condition called Symmetrical Lupoid Onchodystrophy or for short SLO. SLO is a painful condition whereby the external nails of the dog split and begin to peel backwards, until eventually the nail drops off altogether. Not only is this very painful while it happens but the resulting split nails and swollen sore paw pads are then left highly susceptible to infection. The condition is worsened in dry cold weather and by the dog walking on concrete or similar ground underfoot. The condition meant that Macgyver had to give up his work as a pat dog and long walks in his favourite parks became limited in order to keep him on the soft ground only.

SLO is well known as being very tough to treat His owner Sophi, was informed by the veterinary dermatologist that the conventional veterinary routewas to rather optimistically treat him with pharmaceutical grade vitamin and mineral supplements.

The dermatologist recommended also consulting a holistic vet. It was this Vet that proposed Sophi consider switching Macgyver's diet over to one that contained raw meat and vegetables. It made sense to Sophi as the treatments so far had centered around getting more nutrients, especially minerals into his system. A diet that promised a greater digestibility and bio availability of nutrients was worth a try. In Sophi's words 'the diet has made a massive difference to him! Since beginning his new feeding regime of pre packed raw meat, ground bone and vegetables he has only had one occurrence of a nail split, during a particularly dry cold spell around February last year. I can't praise the new diet enough and have recommended it to almost all my clients since!

Macgyver is back to his old self and enjoying life to the maximum, we hope that in time he will be able to head back into the hospitals to share some of his love and affection again.

www.doghollow.co.uk

Is it such a raw deal?

Jez Rose - Canine Behaviour Specialist

I began feeding a raw diet to my own dogs after meeting Dr. Tom Lonsdale, the veterinarian credited with first popularising feeding a natural, raw diet to pet dogs back in the early nineties.

I was a little sceptical, however, the scientist in me was intrigued and it did make sense. I did not remain sceptical for long, however, as I began to see the results of a natural diet within a matter of days: a shinier coat that people commented on, softer fur, whiter teeth, no halitosis and less fecal output. The dogs seemed to enjoy the diet more than commercial food and I felt better for giving them something that seemed more natural to them. Canines are, after all, carnivores.

However, they are also extremely adaptive, as are their digestive enzymes. Raw feeding isn't for everyone and if the thought of throwing your dog an entire dead rabbit turns your stomach, why not try with simply a bone from the butchers in place of one of their daily meals? Something like a cow's femur with all the tasty bone marrow and nutrients. As well as the many health benefits, it seems to have benefits for behaviour and temperament, too. Although anecdotal, myself and other professionals have noticed more attentive behaviour (arguably more willing to learn) and a reduction in hyperactivity. I see in the region of two hundred and fifty clients each year and recommend a raw diet to all of them – those that have tried it continue to feed raw and are full of praise for the physical and behavioural changes seen in their dogs. I believe feeding a raw diet may well improve reactive dogs: dogs that bark or lunge at other dogs or people. This is anecdotal and I believe there is yet to be any research into the impact a raw diet has on behaviour, however, it would appear that those dogs fed a raw diet are somewhat calmer. Although feeding a raw diet certainly doesn't "cure" reactivity, in those dogs my practice has worked with, it certainly seemed that switching to a raw diet helped to progress quicker and owners did notice a difference in the dog's behaviour.

It would make sense that if the dog is being fed a natural diet that does not cause discomfort and provides natural nutrients and energy, then their behaviour is going to be directly impacted by this. Chef Jamie Oliver proved with his hugely successful and Government backed school dinners campaign, that input directly effects output: feed additives, manufactured sugars and other nasties and you have children that suddenly have a propensity to draw on walls and run around screaming a lot. The same is true of any living species – a sort of "what we eat, we become" philosophy.

Further anecdotal evidence would be found in that, of all the dogs I have come into contact with or trained, many of the problems associated with some commercial foods like excessive drinking, hyperactivity, anxiety and excessive urination are hardly ever seen in those dogs fed by a raw diet and when they are seen, changing the diet has not improved it, suggesting the problem was pathological, not diet.

www.JezRose.co.uk

What I Feed My Dogs for nutritional benefit and economical value

by Bob Weatherwax

Hollywood dog trainer and owner/breeder/trainer of the Lassie film and television Collies Everything I first knew about nutrition, I learned from my father, Rudd, who learned from his father, Walter. My dad grew up on a working angora goat farm in the sparse mountainous part of New Mexico. In those days – the last years of the 19th century and first part of the 20th – farms were mainly self-sustaining. Everything and everybody had a purpose, from livestock and crops to family members. As a boy, my surroundings reminded me of the children's nursery rhyme, Old MacDonald Had a Farm. We seemed to have at least one or more of every animal you'd find in a barn or pasture. I soon understood why. Coming out of the Depression years and heading straight into World War II rationing, no matter how well my dad's career as a Hollywood dog trainer went, he always thought about economy first while maintaining the best value. His approach was most obvious in the recipe he concocted to feed the 40 to 60 dogs in the kennel. Every dog had to be in top condition, ready to appear in the background of a scene or lead the action in a scene. From our chickens, eggs – shell and all – went into the recipe. From our goats and cows, milk was added. Meat from a butchered pig or cow or goat or chicken was a major ingredient. Whatever the livestock ate vegetables, fruit, grain – often found its way into the recipe. Bones were not a part of the recipe since the whole concoction was cooked up. But times and attitudes changed. My father and I both fed canned and bagged food to our dogs while adding a modified version of the recipe now and then. Who couldn't say no to the convenience that commercial food promotes!

About ten years ago, I became aware of the new trend to feed raw. It made sense to me. Some people may think that's going backwards – back to a simpler time and back when convenience wasn't available. But in giving my dog's home-prepared food again and raw meat and bones, I noticed an incredible difference. I always considered my Hollywood working dogs to be healthy and long-lived, but on a diet of real whole fresh food, their coat texture and coat length were more correct, their eyes sparkled, their responsiveness and alertness were magnified, and their teeth gleamed. Oh, there is one other way I could tell how nutritious this diet was. It was crystal clear that what the dogs ate was really being absorbed and used healthily. The size and amount of waste material was greatly re!duced. Yard pickup never went so easy or so fast

Now that I have moved away from Hollywood and am no longer active in training dogs for the entertainment industry, my own dogs – my personal pets –continue to reap the benefits of this easy to prepare diet. For a while, I lived right at the edge of a man-made lake stocked with fish. I'd get my rod and reel, my dogs would follow me, and, as soon as I'd catch a fish, the dogs would grab their treat and devour it. Now, I shop for their meals in the same markets that I shop for my meals. For the most part, I follow a prey diet for my two young dogs, who eat raw turkey and raw chicken. The big dog loves his turkey necks and drumsticks. The little dog loves his chicken necks and wings.

All in all, my expenses for the raw meat and bones are quite reasonable and actually, pound for pound and dollar for dollar, less expensive than canned or bagged dog food. Nutritionally speaking, my dogs couldn't be healthier. I do make dietary changes for aging dogs, based on the condition of their teeth or other health needs. My last old dog needed a diet that went easy on his mouth and his stomach. For him, I prepared a stew of steamed rice, boiled chicken, and cooked vegetables.

If I've learned one thing in my lifetime, it's the truth behind the saying, "everything old is new again." These days, we talk about the benefits of sustainable farms and local farmers markets – the same values that my dad and grandfather stood by and practiced. These days, we try to stretch our money as far as it will go – just as my dad and grandfather did in the lean times of their lives. And these days, we recognize all over again just how important the human/animal bond is – the very thing that has given my family professional pride and a respected legacy. As for me, I can tell you that I was never happier than when I was in my father's kennel, caring for and playing with the puppies.... then I was just a young pup myself. Nothing has really changed. Now my best moments are the ones I share with my dogs, which includes giving them the best diet possible.

www.weatherwaxtraineddogs.com

Resources

Ready made raw meals for your dog
www.healthful.uk.com – *Delivery and retail stockists.*
www.honeysrealdogfood.com – *UK based, will deliver to most of UK.*
www.k9foryourdog.co.uk – *Deliver in East Anglian area of UK.*
www.k9natural.com/retailers-and-wholesalers – *Worldwide branches, delivery, retail stockists.*
www.naturesmenu.co.uk (frozen raw meals) – *UK delivery and retail stockists.*
www.omaspride.com – *Distributors and delivery all over USA.*
www.pawnatraw.com – *USA, retail stockists.*
www.thedogfoodcompany.co.uk – *Delivery to some of UK.*

Find yourself a wonderful Holistic Vet
www.ahvma.org – *American Holistic Veterinary Medical Association*
www.abva.co.uk – *Association of British Veterinary Acupuncturists*
www.bahvs.com – *British Association of Homeopathic Veterinary Surgeons*
www.acuvet.com.au – *Australian Veterinary Acupuncture Group*
www.rawfoodvets.com – *A directory of Vets who support and understand raw feeding dogs.*

Miscellaneous
www.canine-health-concern.org.uk – *Charity researching the science behind natural and alternative care for dogs.*
www.facebook.com/NaturallyHealthyDogs – *Regularly updated information and articles on natural dog care.*
www.facebook.com/caninehealth101 – *Information and Science behind raw feeding and holistic dog care.*
www.nataliebardensportraits.co.uk – *Spiritual artist and pet portraiture, capturing personality.*
www.facebook.com/lovewoofandwonder – *spiritual dog ownership*
www.tilleyfarm.co.uk – *training centre for the Tellington TTouch*

The products and services listed are for reference only.
No endorsements are made by the authors to the services listed on this page.

Caroline is an animal well-being expert with 18 years experience working with natural pet care and holistic training techniques. Her qualifications as an animal healer, Tellington TTouch pet behaviour practitioner, balance procedure coach & trainer, canine hypnotherapist and nutritional therapist empower owners with a deeper understanding of their animal friends bodies and minds. They allow both pets and their owners the chance to transform relationships, overcome well-being issues, solve behaviour problems and create a happier more peaceful lifestyle.

Caroline is committed to achieving a greater understanding and acceptance of the philosophy and science behind the power of the mind, natural holistic living and of course to teaching compassionate ways we can all understand and improve the lives of our own pets, and animals globally.

Her goal in life is to educate and empower as many people as possible with the knowledge and tools to create a more peaceful, happier and confident future for animals and pets worldwide.

Guidelines to 'how much to give' puppies and adult dogs.

Puppies aged 0 – 3 weeks
– should be drinking the mother's milk to obtain essential nutrients, enzymes and essential fatty acids.

Puppies aged 3 – 4 weeks
- Pups need 3 meals a day. Feed around 8% of the puppy's body weight per day. Mash the foods up very well. If the pups are not still drinking milk from their mother try adding Goats milk to their diet too, as this is very easy for puppies to digest and full of nutrients. Puppies need a little help digesting their foods at this stage, sometime is it better for them to have the feeds 'lightly' cooked. This will mimic the regurgitation that mother dogs provide for their pups in the wild, making the food more digestible for them.

Puppies aged 6 weeks
- At this stage you can begin to introduce a small amount of raw bone within the meal, for instance as chicken wings. No actual raw bones just yet. Most pups will begin to wean from their mother at 3/4 weeks and be weaned completely at 7/8 weeks. They will still benefit from some mothers milk even up to 12 weeks old, if she has any milk left, or any tolerance left to feed them!

Puppies aged over 12 weeks (3 months)
-Feed 2 meals a day, you should be able to feed all the variety of adult raw foods by this stage. Introduce raw meaty bones now too.

Puppies aged over 4 months
-Begin to reduce the amount the puppy eats per day. Aiming to reach 6% of body weight and then 4% by the time the puppy is 6 months old.

Continue to gradually reduce the % of food your puppy eats as he grows up. Dropping from 4% of his body weight per day to 3% and then down to 2% by the time he is a year old.

As mentioned in the How much to give chapter, I know many owners of large breed dogs who only feed 1% or 1.5% of body weight per day and their dogs thrive on this amount. The guidelines are just that, guidelines and are best tailored to fit the activity levels, health, metabolism, lifestyle and importantly breed size of your dog, as an individual.

Notes

Notes

7769932R00028

Printed in Great Britain
by Amazon.co.uk, Ltd.,
Marston Gate.